Laughing at Funerals

FINDING THE GOOD AND THE GOD
IN LIFE'S UPS AND DOWNS

Katherine Smith Bryant

*To Jessica Phillips—
May you always find
the joy + work to pass
it on!
Katherine Bryant
Matthew 5:16*

For Queenie-

Who taught me more about life and love

than I ever realized

Introduction

As you might can imagine, living in a house with four boys comes with its fair share of surprises. I have found race cars in the dryer, rocks in every nook and cranny you can think of, and a 2-foot long snakeskin in a camp trunk. That one about gave me a heart attack! Once, I even found a bag of liquefied salad in the pot holder drawer, and yes, it was every bit as disgusting as you're imagining.

But none of those discoveries prepared me for the morning I opened my freezer and came face to face with a pair of muddy, smelly baseball pants just chillin' on top of my Eggo waffles. I mean, they could have been on top of the onions or the salmon—you know, things that are stinky by nature—but no, they were on top of my precious Eggos, and that's just rude.

After watching me put the boys through the Inquisition as I demanded answers for this heinous crime, Alex calmly confessed he was the culprit, explaining freezing clothes is the perfect solution when your son sits in a ginormous, sticky blob of Big League Chew. Huh, who knew? Alex really surprises me with his laundry expertise sometimes.

When I started my blog, Laughs at Funerals, in 2017, I didn't mean for it to turn into devotional posts. It started as observations about parenting, marriage, and friendship, with a little humor thrown in every now and then. After a few years of writing, though, I noticed my posts started to turn toward Jesus.

And honestly, I fought the shift. I didn't feel in any way qualified to write about God and tell people about Jesus. I mean, I mess up every day. I yell at my boys, I've been known to sleep through my quiet time on more than one occasion, and, thanks to social media, I may or may not have coveted my neighbor's donkey . . . especially when that donkey is actually a vacation in Turks and Caicos. In other words, I didn't feel like I had any authority to proclaim the Good News.

But here's the thing—God loves a mess. The messier the mess, the better because it gives God a greater chance to shine as He turns the mess into a miracle. Some of the biggest sinners and scoundrels in the Bible—sorry, Paul, but you know it's true—became some of the most impactful messengers for God. He uses each one of us, sins and all, to tell His story.

What I've learned over the past few years is that God shows up at unexpected times in unexpected places in unexpected ways. He sees more than we see and knows more than we know. He's a miracle worker, a promise keeper, and ultimately, a loving savior. He can take a muddy pair of baseball pants and make them white as snow, and He doesn't even need Fels Naptha to do it.

And so, that's my prayer for each of you as you read these devotions, that you see God in everyday moments. Life is full of ups and downs, but it shouldn't surprise us that God is present in both, we just have to pay attention. We can find comfort in His presence and hope in His promises. God loves us and is always near us, and I hope that's what sticks with you.

Laughs at Funerals

As the Father has loved me, so have I loved you. Now remain in my love. If you keep my commands, you will remain in my love, just as I have kept my Father's commands and remain in his love. I have told you this so that my joy may be in you and that your joy may be complete.

John 15:9-11

Have you ever read through dating ads in the classifieds? People write little lines like *Enjoys long walks on the beach*, *Wants to see the world*, or *Must love dogs* to sum up who they are in 100 characters or less. After a great deal of thought, I've decided if I ever need a dating ad, my tagline will be *Laughs at funerals*.

That's right. My name is Katherine Bryant, and I laugh at inappropriate times.

It's a problem I've been cursed with my whole life.

My husband is actually the one who suggested I name my blog *Laughs at Funerals* because, as he claims, it perfectly explains who I am. He meant it as a compliment . . . I think. And bless him, he's had plenty of experience with my inappropriate laughter. I mean, I laughed in his face when he proposed! Now wait a minute, before you go feeling all sorry for him. He should have known what to expect—I laughed the first time he kissed me too.

As inappropriate as that laughter was, no experience can top the time I laughed at my dear friend's grandmother's funeral. That's right, while everyone was wiping away tears, I was trying with all my might to suppress the full-on belly laugh that was trying to escape. The worst part was, the madder my mom got at me for laughing, the harder I laughed, and pretty soon the whole pew was shaking. That sentence makes it sound like I was a little kid when this happened . . . I was 21.

Seriously, though, I had a good reason to laugh. In the middle of the service, a fond memory of the deceased popped into my head, and all I could picture was her in a camisole, hanging out of a bathroom window, flagging me down so I could knock on the front door and tell her husband and son, who were both oblivious to her incessant banging, she was locked in the upstairs bathroom.

So I got tickled.

So sue me.

But think about it. Is laughing at a funeral really that bad? After all, shouldn't we be celebrating life and the person we love? In the craziness of the daily grind, it's easy to get caught up in the negative. I'll admit, it can be difficult to find the joy in some situations. In those times, we may just have to fake it 'til we make it because the bottom line is life is short, and we only get one chance to live it the way we want to. I don't know about you, but I want to live my life so that at my funeral, people will remember that I laughed, that I found joy.

As Christians, we are called to be joyful. In fact, the words *joy*, *joyful*, and *rejoice* appear in the Bible over 430 times combined. So, the question is how do we find joy in the midst of grief and hardship? The short answer is easy: Jesus. If we make Jesus' joy our own, it will never leave us. His joy and His love are constant and never change, no matter what we're going through. Jesus' steadfast nature is more than enough reason to rejoice.

In terms of my inappropriate laughter, I would like to say I've gotten better, that I no longer laugh at the wrong time or in the wrong place, but that would be a lie. Just know, if you fall, I'll help you up, but I'll be laughing all the way. After all, it's (kinda) what God called me to do.

Distracted By a Donkey

"Come," he said.

Then Peter got down out of the boat, walked on the water and came toward Jesus. But when he saw the wind, he was afraid and, beginning to sink, cried out, "Lord, save me!"

Immediately Jesus reached out his hand and caught him. "You of little faith," he said, "why did you doubt?"

Matthew 14: 29-31

Every year on Christmas Eve, our church has a live nativity as a part of the Christmas Eve service. We start in the sanctuary, and as the Christmas story is read, various characters join the scene. In 2018, Alex, Brooks, and I had the honor of being Mary, Joseph, and Baby Jesus, while Jackson and Reeves were excited to be shepherds.

The best part of the night is always after the service when the nativity moves to the front lawn of the church, and we bring out the live animals: sheep, cows, and a camel. In 2018, the scene even included a baby donkey. Now, I don't know if you've ever seen a baby donkey, but let me tell you, they are super cute.

Yet, as I watched everyone "ooh" and "ahh" over this baby donkey, I started to get annoyed . . . and maybe even a little jealous. I mean, there I was, holding the Christ child—played by the cutest baby ever, if I do say so myself—and nobody was paying us any attention. All eyes were on that dumb donkey.

I turned to Alex and complained, "Man, Al, they're looking at the wrong baby!"

And then it hit me. How often do I look at the wrong baby? How often am I the one who loses focus? How often do I take my eyes off of Jesus?

Let's be real—it's easy to get distracted in today's world. I get preoccupied by social media, episodes of my favorite TV shows, and good books, just to name a few. This week alone, I've been so wrapped up in helping the boys make their valentines, I've completely neglected my Bible study.

Even when I try to focus on Jesus, my mind often wanders. I start to pray, and the next thing I know, I'm making my grocery list. Or, I start reading a devotion on my phone, and before long, I'm Googling why Cardi B. was so mad after the Grammy's, she shut down her Instagram account.

I have good intentions, but I end up going down the rabbit hole, and pretty soon, Jesus is the last thing on my mind. And that's when things start to get rough.

The boys love the story of Peter walking on water. Reeves thinks of him as a superhero with special powers, kinda like Aquaman, I guess. And while there is special power going on in the story, it's not coming from Peter.

In Matthew's story, Peter, a little skeptical of Jesus' appearance on the lake, asks to walk on the water toward him. Things are going great for Peter . . . until he takes his eyes off of Jesus. When he looks at the wind, he becomes afraid and starts to sink. Immediately, Jesus reaches out his hand and saves Peter.

I can feel the same thing happening to me when I pay more attention to everything swirling around me instead of focusing on Jesus. I start to feel overwhelmed, like I'm drowning in my to-do list, my commitments, my fears. But when I take time to just sit and be still, to listen to a favorite hymn, to read and study the Bible, I get a sense of calm, a feeling of peace. He saves me from drowning in all that "stuff" when I turn my eyes to Him.

My distractions change from day to day, but, thankfully, God doesn't change. He's always there, constant and consistent, waiting for me to regain my focus.

The live nativity was a fun experience for my whole family, one I hope the boys will always remember. But for me, it was more than that. For me, the memory reminds me to stay focused on the right baby all year long.

Dodge, Duck, Dip, Dive, & Deuteronomy

> *Then I said to you, "Do not be terrified; do not be afraid of them. The* LORD *your God, who is going before you, will fight for you, as he did for you in Egypt, before your very eyes, and in the wilderness. There you saw how the* LORD *your God carried you, as a father carries his son, all the way you went until you reached this place."*

Deuteronomy 1:29-31

What.A.Week.

With a half day, Election Day, and an eLearning day at school, plus baseball games, speech therapy, a church committee meeting, and Alex being out of town, life has been a wee bit crazy over the past five days.

To be honest, my whole fall has been a tad overwhelming. There have been times I have felt like I'm in a game of dodgeball, where I'm the only one left on my side, and all of these balls keep flying at me, and there's nothing I can do to fight them off or make them stop pummeling me. Some days, I'd really rather just curl into a ball with my arms over my head and wait until things settle down, but I know deep down that's not the way to win at dodgeball . . . or at life.

Patches O'Houlihan, the greatest dodgeball coach of all time, would tell me the way to win in dodgeball is to utilize the five D's: dodge, duck, dip, dive, and dodge. And those moves may help a team of average Joes win the Las Vegas Dodgeball Championship, but they don't really enable me to conquer the challenges, responsibilities, and occasional wrenches coming at me every day.

What Patches' advice forgets is that one of the best strategies to win at dodgeball is to actually stand still, catch a ball, hold onto it, and use it to fend off the other balls. And the ball we specifically need to grab onto is the one with God's name on it.

See, we can duck and dive, dip and dodge, cower and cover our heads, but that doesn't stop the hailstorm of life that is raining down on us. When we stand up and cling tightly to Jesus, though, that's when we can start taking care of business.

Throughout the Psalms, God is compared to a shield, which I'm sure was helpful to the Israelites who were used to going into battle, but it doesn't do too much for me in modern-day America. I don't know a lot about BC-era weaponry, but dodgeballs? As a mom, a teacher with recess duty, and a former camp counselor, that's an analogy I can really get behind. (See what I did there?) To me, God is a dodgeball, going before me, protecting me, and giving me something to hold on to.

I'm fairly certain a dodgeball was exactly what Moses was thinking of when he wrote Deuteronomy 1:30: *The Lord your God, who is going before you, will fight for you, as he did for you in Egypt, before your very eyes.*

Moses was reminding his people that they weren't alone. They had seen God bring them through hard times, through droughts and plagues and crazy pharaohs chasing after them, and Moses wanted them to remember God was still walking before them.

The same is true for us today. Life throws tough stuff at us, but we never have to handle it by ourselves. God is always on our side. He is our first line of defense, shielding us and helping us manage everything that comes our way.

So, when you're feeling overwhelmed, grab on to God. Hold him out in front of you and let him protect you.

He can. He has. He will.

Worth the Wait

Let us not become weary in doing good, for at the proper time we will reap a harvest if we do not give up.

Galatians 6:9

Thanks to impending bad weather, yesterday was a traumatic day for a lot of parents in and around Columbia, as we were thrust back into the chaos that is eLearning. For many of us, the day brought back horrific memories of throwing tantrums, slamming doors, and cussing, and I'm only referring to my own personal behavior during Covid school.

To be fair, Jackson's eLearning experience in 2020 wasn't completely scarring. He was in the third grade and could do a lot of his work independently. But Reeves'? Reeves' experience made me wonder how early was too early for a mimosa.

I felt like every day with Reeves was a disaster. Because he was only in first grade at the time, he needed a lot of help, and understandably so. Problem was, so did the 85 students on the other end of my own Teams meetings, and since I couldn't figure out how to balance teaching and parenting, most days Reeves just rolled around on the floor, did handstands on the furniture, and made 12-foot long snakes out of tape and construction paper. Let's just say, it wasn't quite the standards-based experience I was hoping for.

By mid-September, I was so stressed and frazzled, I lost my temper and yelled . . . a lot. And neither did much to help nurture a little boy who wasn't really a fan of school to begin with. Just when I thought I couldn't do it anymore and had resigned myself to the fact that we'd have a first grade dropout in the family, the clouds parted and a nearby private school opened another first grade class. Reeves got a spot where he could go to school face to face every day and run around on the playground with his friends. He also got a teacher who saw him in person in the classroom for seven hours a day and who started asking good questions about his attention and his work habits.

What we would soon discover is that Reeves has ADHD. The past two school years have been full of ups and downs as we have returned to our original elementary school and have worked to help Reeves rekindle his love of learning and figure out how he can be successful in school. Yet, even though this year has been his best year by far, I was still apprehensive about returning to a virtual system that brought back so many bad memories, even if only for one day.

So imagine my surprise yesterday morning when I walked into the kitchen and saw Reeves sitting at the table, calmly filling out his weather observation chart, completely unprompted. The sight literally stopped me in my tracks. It was a total 180 from where we were two years ago.

Now, I know that two years can make a huge difference in a student's life, especially when it involves learning to read independently. And I also know that medication and therapy have done a lot to help Reeves maintain his focus and lessen his anxiety.

But I'd be lying to myself and to you if I didn't acknowledge the part God played in all of this. He has blessed us with the right schools at the right times, with teachers who encourage all of us daily, and with friends who have prayed with us through the trials and the triumphs.

As I stared at Reeves in awe, I couldn't help but think of one of my favorite Bible verses. Galatians 6:9 says, "Let us not become weary in doing good, for at the proper time we will reap a harvest if we do not give up."

It's hard to remember this truth when we're in the weeds of parenting. When it seems like every day brings a new challenge, a new struggle. I'll be honest, I have wanted to throw in the towel more than once over the past two years. There were days I felt like therapy was a waste of time and money. We tried four different medications before we found the right one. Nothing was a quick fix. But God knows parenting is a marathon, not a sprint. He's in it for the long haul, and He knows raising children is going to take time. I guess that's why He gives them to us for 18 years instead of just eight.

Whatever parenting or life struggle you're facing, keep going. Whether it's helping your teenager manage peer pressure and friendships or constantly reminding your four year old that hands are not for hitting, keep fighting the good fight. Keep leaning into God and putting faith in His promises.

Seeing Reeves happily working away at the table was just the reminder I needed that the harvest we long for is worth the wait.

The Bigger, the Better

In him and through faith in him we may approach God with freedom and confidence.

Ephesians 3:12

As a parent, I've discovered there are a few things I can never have too much of. I can never have too much athletic wear or too many wet wipes. I can never have too much patience or too many Goldfish. And, above all, I can never have too much wisdom.

This has been especially evident the past few months as we have tried to help Brooks get used to "big boy school." It hasn't been easy, and we have relied heavily on the wisdom of friends and experts. Thanks to a Sunday school lesson a few weeks ago that focused on James 1:5, we have also started to rely on God's wisdom.

Last week, Alex and I prayed for wisdom for what to do next, for guidance, and for clarity. I went on to pray for all of the adults in Brooks' life to have wisdom for the best ways to help him as well.

Alex chuckled at the second half of my prayer, telling me he didn't think I could pray for other people to have wisdom, to which I very maturely replied, "Yes, I can. I can pray for whatever I want."

They say my stubbornness is genetic.

But seriously, in Psalm 109, David, a man after God's own heart, asks for his enemy's days to be few. Then he asks for his enemy's children to be fatherless, so I think asking for adults I respect to be blessed with wisdom is actually pretty kind and compassionate, comparatively speaking.

Later that morning as I was driving to school, I thanked God for being a God who listens and for being a God who lets me ask for a wide variety of things . . . and that's when it hit me.

Isn't that what we all want? To be asked?

Think about it . . .

Do we actually want to chair the fall festival at school? No, probably not, but it sure feels good to be asked.

Do we honestly want to go on a blind date with our best friend's quirky cousin from out of town? Chances are not really, but it sure feels good to be asked.

Do we seriously want to single-handedly organize a field trip, complete with spreadsheets and permission slips? Nope, not even a little bit, but (say it with me) it sure feels good to be asked.

If we don't have any interest in completing the task, why does it still feel good to be asked? It's simple: Being asked shows us someone believes in our ability, thinks we're capable, and needs our help. Ultimately, it means someone trusts us, and that feels good.

God wants the same thing from us too, a relationship where we feel comfortable enough to share our deepest desires, our hopes, and our dreams. A relationship where we trust His ability and rely on His help. He wants us to ask Him anything because it brings us closer to Him.

Now look, I'm not saying we're going to get everything we ask for. God isn't Zoltar, ready to grant *Big* wishes. But He is willing to *listen* to everything we ask for.

John 9:31 tells us that "if anyone is a worshipper of God and does his will, God listens to him" (ESV). Paul expands on this idea in Ephesians 3:12 when he writes, "in him [Jesus] we may approach God with freedom and confidence."

In other words, we don't have to worry about what we ask God for because He's not going to judge us or laugh at us or get angry with us. He's going to listen to us like the good father He is. And, I would imagine, God will be excited we finally had enough faith in His ability to ask Him to do something for us He's wanted to do all along.

So, as you talk to God today, go ahead and be bold in your asking. Go big! Be honest with God, and be honest with yourself.

You have nothing to lose and so much to gain.

Call Me... Maybe?

The one who calls you is faithful, and he will do it.

I Thessalonians 5:24

"Get in the car, guys! We're running late! Hurry! Hurry!"

That's how July 30, 2021, started for us as Reeves, Brooks, and I scrambled to get in the car. We were heading to Asbury Hills to pick Jackson up from camp, and we were way behind schedule. I had loaded the boys into my trusty Pilot and was climbing into the front seat when my phone rang.

Now, as a general rule, I detest talking on the phone and avoid it whenever possible. My friends know this about me, and on more than one occasion, I've answered the phone to the words, "I know you don't like talking on the phone, but this will just take a sec." Answering the phone when I was already stressed from running late was totally out of character for me.

When I glanced down at the caller ID, I saw it was my friend Margaret, who likes to play fast and loose with my "Don't call me, I'll call you" rule anyway. I don't know what possessed me, but I answered the phone, even though I was cranking my car and trying to hit the road. And, man, was I glad I did. Turned out, I was only *trying* to crank my car. My trusty Pilot was dead as a doornail. How were we going to get to Jackson?

In a panic, I relayed this untimely development to Margaret, and Margaret being Margaret, she immediately offered to let me borrow her car, a sweet Honda Odyssey van complete with a DVD player and push-button start—fancy! With self-closing doors, *Jungle 2 Jungle* on the big screen, and captain's chairs, the boys were in heaven. Best.RoadTrip.Ever. To think, we would have missed out on all of the fun, not to mention picking up Jackson, if I hadn't answered the phone.

Sometimes I wonder if I'm doing the same thing with God. Am I ignoring His calls?

The short answer is yes.

I have put God on hold and sent Him to voicemail more than I'd like to admit. But that's the great thing about God. He is, quite possibly, the most obnoxious and annoying telemarketer ever. He keeps on calling. Even when I try to ignore God because I'm too busy or too scared to talk, He doesn't give up. He keeps calling.

As Paul writes in I Thessalonians 5:24, *The one who calls you is faithful, and he will do it.* And aren't we thankful that He is and He does? Imagine the blessings we wouldn't experience if God never hit redial. The best part is we can have faith that if He calls, He will equip us with what we need to answer.

What is God calling you to do? Is it to take that first step or mend that relationship? Is it to reach out to an old friend or try something new? Is it to extend an invitation or put an idea into action? Whatever it is, let's make a pact to answer when God calls us. It may be scary at first, and it may require us to step out of our comfort zones, but we may be pleasantly surprised by all the good things that follow when we pick up the phone, so to speak.

So, what are you waiting for? Your phone is ringing. Answer the call.

Shedding the Old

Because of the LORD's great love we are not consumed, for his compassions never fail. They are new every morning; great is your faithfulness.

Lamentations 3:22-23

On the last day of school, Jackson brought home a lot of things: a bunch of old notebooks, brand new novels for summer reading, and . . . the class pet, Spot. Before you start feeling sorry for me for enduring three months of feeding a lizard mealworms twice a day, there's something you should know: I brought this on myself.

Back in January, Jackson came home from a friend's house telling me all about his friend's leopard gecko and begging me to get him one. I politely declined his request and went on about my business.

A few weeks later, Jackson's class was voting on what they should get as a class pet, and in a moment of pure genius, I emailed his teacher and asked if there were anything I could do to ensure the leopard gecko won the vote. I figured if Jackson had a gecko at school, he wouldn't need one at home. And what do you know, the gecko won! I was basking in the glory of my ingenuity when his teacher sent a follow-up email, asking if I would help her out and house the gecko over the summer, you know, since she had helped me out with the vote and all. Well played, Mrs. B, well played. I definitely didn't see that coming.

And thus, on June 3, Spot became our new pet.

One day toward the end of the first week, I noticed Spot was looking a little lethargic and ashen. Worried Spot was depressed in his new habitat, I shared my concern with Jackson. I mean, I may not have wanted Spot in my house, but I sure wasn't going to let him kick the bucket on my watch.

Jackson reassured me that everything was ok, Spot was just turning white because he was getting ready to shed.

I'm sorry, what now? I didn't sign on for shedding. That sounded a little too similar to those legless reptiles I avoid at all cost.

"Are you serious?" I sputtered.

Jackson, thinking he was helping the situation, nonchalantly replied, "Oh, but we don't have to clean it up. Spot eats it."

Y'all, I thought I was going to lose my lunch!

Reeves, who was by this time rolling on his bed with laughter at my visible distress, took a breath long enough to tell me it was "nutritious." To which Jackson added, "Don't worry, Mom, he'll do it at night when no one is watching."

Oh, well, why didn't you say so. What good manners Spot has.

The funny thing is even though I was thoroughly grossed out by this turn of events, I couldn't help but think of 2 Corinthians 5:7: *Therefore, if anyone is in Christ, the new creation has come: The old has gone, the new is here!*

Just goes to show you, God has a sense of humor and can send us a message through just about any situation if we pay attention.

The boys were right. Geckos shed their skin every four to eight weeks and come out more vibrant and energetic on the other side.

The same is true for us. When we give our hearts to God, we can shed the guilt and shame of previous failures and mistakes and come out brighter and full of life. We don't have to cling to the past. Being in Christ nourishes our souls, taking what has grown dull and making it shiny and new.

The good news for us is we don't have to wait four to eight weeks to start anew. God's mercies are new every morning (Lamentations 3:22-23), and we have the ability to ask for forgiveness as often as we need it. And unlike my reaction of creepy disgust, God is never turned off by who we are. He simply wants us to come to Him so that we may be renewed by His grace and refreshed in His love.

So, even though Spot still kinda gives me the heebie geebies, I do have an appreciation for him. After all, he reminds me of a very important truth.

May we all remember that, like Spot, we always have the opportunity for a fresh start, a new beginning in Christ.

Eating My Words

The words of the reckless pierce like swords, but the tongue of the wise brings healing.

Proverbs 12:18

We're all familiar with the saying, "Sticks and stones will break my bones, but words will never hurt me." But let's be honest—that's a lie. Words can be just as hurtful as sticks and stones, and their scars can be even harder to heal.

Recently, Reeves had a meltdown as Alex was tucking him into bed. He had had a rough night, where nothing seemed to go right for him. He was especially upset because earlier in the evening, he had spilled a drink all over the carpet in the hall. As Alex was telling me about the situation, he said, "Poor guy even said he's the reason we can't have nice things."

Cue record scratch.

I immediately felt horrible because I knew exactly where Reeves had gotten that idea and those words—ME.

As you can imagine, a house with four guys has its fair share of rips, spills, and cracks. To maintain my sanity, sometimes all I can do is shake my head and chuckle, "That's why Mama can't have nice things." I've even been tempted to buy a pillow with the saying embroidered on it. Little did I know, Reeves was internalizing those words much more than I ever meant for him to.

It hurt my mama heart knowing I had hurt his, but that knowledge was also a blessing in disguise. It gave me the opportunity to make it right.

Proverbs 12:18 says, *The words of the reckless pierce like swords, but the tongue of the wise brings healing.*

We don't always know when our words have hurt someone, but when we do, we should use our wisdom to apologize. As uncomfortable as the conversation may be, it's worth it to bring healing to the relationship.

Apologizing to our children is especially important, as it models for them how to treat others. It's good practice at a skill that doesn't always come naturally. While it can be intimidating to humble ourselves and admit when we're wrong, it can also be a character-building learning experience for everyone involved.

I've decided I don't want our family motto to be "This is why we can't have nice things." I'd rather it be something more along the lines of "In our house, we apologize." Or, "In our house, we take ownership for our mistakes." Or, better yet, "In our house, we know words have the power to heal."

Now that's something to put on a pillow.

Come to Me

Because of the LORD's great love we are not consumed, for his compassions never fail. They are new every morning; great is your faithfulness.

Matthew 11:28-30

Over Spring Break, Alex and I took the boys to Atlanta for a few days to see the sights and catch a Braves game. The morning of the game, Alex had a work emergency, and instead of losing my mind trying to stop the boys from jumping bed to bed playing Floor Is Lava while Alex sent emails and made calls, I thought I would be a supportive wife and take the boys to Truist Park all by myself, and Alex could work in peace and then Uber to meet us there, easy breezy.

Fun Fact: It was neither easy, nor breezy.

What started out as a loving wife taking care of her family quickly turned into a maniac driver gripping the steering wheel so tightly her knuckles turned white.

I got us to the stadium without too much trouble, but then we had to park. Talk about a nightmare! There were all of these different colored lots, and they all seemed to require passes, which we didn't have.

I kept driving, thinking we'd come to a pay-to-park lot, but they were all full. We were getting farther and farther from the stadium when we finally saw a lot for $60. At this point, I would have paid $600, but unfortunately, I only had $20 cash. So we found an ATM at a QT, maxed out my debit card to be on the safe side, and headed back to the lot, but now we were on the wrong side of the road, and I couldn't turn left.

Instead, we were stuck in a lane heading back to the interstate.

At that point, I was ready to head back to the hotel and watch the game on the 32" TV. It would be totally the same, right?

The whole time I was driving in circles, the boys kept asking a million questions and saying, "We've already passed this." It was like in *Speed* when the guy on the bus says, "We're at the airport? I've already seen the airport." I was yelling. Jackson was crying. We were miserable. Overwhelmed, scared, and frustrated, all I wanted was for someone to take the wheel and just get us there already.

Alex, who by this time had finished his work and Ubered to the stadium (because of course he had), called to check on us, and I straight up hung up on him. The boys were horrified, but I couldn't manage talking on the phone and navigating a gagillion lanes of traffic. Plus, I irrationally blamed Alex for my predicament and was livid he seemed to have bebopped to the game without a care in the world. Admittedly, not my finest moment.

At a stop light, I texted him, "I can't get us there."

He immediately sent me the pin of his location and a text that said, "Come to me."

I texted back, "OTW," and he replied, "I'll be here."

In that instant, I felt an incredible weight lift off my shoulders and my heart rate slow down. I was able to get us right to the parking garage where Alex had saved us a space, and the attendants even washed our car during the game. Talk about a miracle.

And isn't that the way it is with God? We don't have to cry and cuss and go around in circles because we always know where He is; His pin never changes. He offers an open invitation to come to Him. He waits for us, no matter how long it takes, no matter what we have to go through, no matter what shape we're in when we finally arrive. He is always ready to welcome us, we just have to give up our plans and surrender to His.

I was worried that my whole breakdown had ruined the day, but it didn't. As soon as the boys saw Alex, they were delighted to tell him that "Mom said bad words!" I was delighted those words were only *crap*, *idiot*, and *freakin'*. Trust me—in my head, I was saying much, MUCH worse.

Not only did we end up having the best time at the game, but I learned an important lesson: When we go crazy, God stays calm. When we get lost, He finds us.

I don't know what your relationship with your earthly father is like, but thankfully, we have a heavenly father who calls out to us when we're lost and confused. God always has room for us, and He doesn't require any sort of special pass. The exorbitant fee has already been paid. He is steady and secure, a good father, welcoming us to rest in Him. All we have to do is accept His grace.

What a gift.

Life GOOOOALS!

The Lord said to him, "Who gave human beings their mouths? Who makes them deaf or mute? Who gives them sight or makes them blind? Is it not I, the Lord? Now go; I will help you speak and will teach you what to say."

Exodus 4:11-12

All of this World Cup hoopla has me reliving my glory days as a high school soccer coach.

Yep, I know what's going through your head right now. Some of you are confused, thinking that's a typo, that I really meant to write about my time as a high school tennis coach. After all, that's the sport I actually played in high school and know something about.

But no, I really did have a short stint as a JV soccer coach . . . and it was as comical as you might imagine.

If you're questioning who in their right mind would hire a soccer coach who didn't know the difference between a free kick and a penalty kick, I don't blame you. That's a fair question. Desperate times call for desperate measures, I suppose.

It's not an exaggeration to say that when I started coaching at Mid-Carolina, I knew less about soccer than Ted Lasso did when he took the reins at Richmond. But, like Ted, what I lacked in soccer knowledge and ability, I more than made up for in my propensity for baking delicious treats for the team.

Honestly, though, no one had any delusions of grandeur when I agreed to coach. The varsity coach, the AD, and I all knew going in I was basically hired to be a warm body in order for us to start a JV team. I wasn't offended in the least, as I was looking forward to getting to know a different group of students. The $100 coaching stipend was just icing on the cake.

When it came time for me to take the field, however, I was pretty anxious, and I worried that my lack of experience would frustrate my players and their parents. Sure, I could blow a whistle and make a bunch of middle schoolers run laps, but I couldn't teach them many soccer skills. #dontuseyourhands

Soon, I realized there was an advantage to my inexperience: Because I knew I wasn't qualified for the job, and I knew I didn't have any idea what I was doing, I didn't put a lot of pressure on myself to have some super impressive record. We celebrated the little victories, and that mindset opened the door for me to learn, to grow, and to laugh at my own mistakes . . . like telling my goal keeper to make a move that resulted in his getting a yellow card—whoopsie daisy!

Bottom line: I may not have been the most able to coach soccer, but I was ready, and I was willing, and that's all my AD needed.

God works in the same way. When He calls us to a job, He just wants us to try. He doesn't expect us to know it all before we start. In fact, I read somewhere recently that God doesn't call the qualified, He qualifies the called.

There are so many leaders in the Bible who started out with a great deal of hesitation. Moses was worried he couldn't speak, Gideon and Saul both felt insignificant because of their families, and Esther feared King Xerxes would never listen to her, a female and a Jew. And yet, despite their feelings of inadequacy, God used each one of these people to do great things.

As Mordecai encourages Esther to go to the king, he asks her, "And who knows but that you have come to your royal position for a time such as this?" (Esther 4:14). In the moment, we don't always know why we're in the position we're in, and we may doubt our ability to be effective. Luckily, God doesn't need our perfection, He needs our obedience, and if we lean into Him, He can use us to fulfill His purpose.

As for my legacy at M-C, did I leave the most impressive record behind when I gave up coaching to work on my Master's . . . absolutely not. But did I help start a JV program that made the varsity program stronger and gave girls the chance to play soccer, eventually leading to the development of their own team . . . why yes, yes I did.

Over my four years of coaching, I learned a lot, and not just how to recognize offside. I learned about teamwork, I learned about motivation, and I learned that I can, in fact, fit in a locker room dryer.

But above all, I learned that we don't have to *be* the best to *give* our best. Sometimes our willingness to try is the key to victory. It's amazing what God can do if we let Him work within us.

All we have to do is BELIEVE.

Put Your Feet Down

I am with you and will watch over you wherever you go, and I will bring you back to this land. I will not leave you until I have done what I have promised you.

Genesis 28:15

Recently, we took a family field trip to Lake Thurmond in Hamilton Branch State Park. It was a fun day of fishing, swimming, and enjoying nature.

At one point, the boys were swimming close to the bank. Brooks had on a life jacket because while Alex has curls like the Hoff, I didn't think he was in the mood for a Baywatch-esque rescue. Brooks loved splashing his brothers and pretending to be a fish in the shallow water.

What was funny was that every time Brooks floated on his stomach, he started to panic, screaming and crying for someone to help him. The first time it happened, we all went over to him, calmly and compassionately explaining to him that he was safe. We showed him he could easily touch the bottom, he just needed to stand up. Five minutes later, he was screaming and crying again. We went over, reminded him what he needed to do, and went back to what we were doing. This cycle continued, and I was beginning to wonder if he had short-term memory loss.

Finally, after about the fourth time, one of us would just yell, "Put your feet down! You can touch!" without even looking his way.

Every time we reminded him he could touch, Brooks would stop flailing, put his feet down on the bottom of the lake, and be like, "Oh, yeah, there it is." We could see the recognition and relief cross his face.

The whole situation reminded me of the story in Matthew 7 of the wise man who built his house on the rock. The rains came down, but his house stayed put because it was on a solid foundation. The foolish man who built his house on the sand wasn't so lucky; his house washed away.

I would wager that fear is the most common storm we face. We can get swept away by the fear of change, of making the wrong choices, of the unknown. We can jump to conclusions and make up worst-case scenarios that will, most likely, never happen. It's so easy to get caught up in the fear of the moment, we toss our rational thinking overboard.

If we have built a relationship with God, though, we always have solid ground to stand on. We don't have to be afraid. We can trust that He will be there to support us through the storms of life. We just have to stop thrashing and splashing long enough to take a breath and remember what's under our feet.

When I'm scared, I act a lot like Brooks. In the midst of my struggles, I often forget how God has helped me in the past. I forget prayers God has answered and miracles He has performed. Ultimately, fear causes me to lose my footing and forget God's promises.

So, how do we reset our feet on the unshakeable foundation of God? Is it through reading the Bible? Going to church? Listening to a favorite song? Talking with a friend? Or even paying attention to the signs of God's presence in our everyday lives? Whatever it is that helps you stay grounded, take time to do it today.

We will all face storms in life, and I'm not gonna lie, some of them may be downright scary. Thankfully, we have a rock to stand on when the rains start coming. Whenever you face fear, my friend, know God is with you and will keep you wherever you go.

All you have to do is put your feet down!

Lesson Learned

Whatever you do, work at it with all your heart, as working for the Lord, not for human masters, since you know that you will receive an inheritance from the Lord as a reward. It is the Lord Christ you are serving.

Colossians 3:23-24

As the school year comes to a close and I reflect on the year, I find myself hoping I imparted at least a little knowledge on my students, even if it was only how to trick the A/C into coming on so we didn't roast in Room 331. I hope my students learned something from being in my class. What's really interesting, though, is sometimes, we don't even realize what we're learning until much, much later.

I remember it like it was yesterday. Jackson brought home his first newsletter from his 3's class at our church's preschool. As I was reading the info, I noticed that the week's memory verse was Colossians 3:23. Not having much faith in a three year old's ability to learn scripture, I asked Jackson if he knew his memory verse.

Jackson looked up at me and, without missing a beat, said: "Whatever you do, work at it with all your heart, as working for the Lord, not for man. Colossians 3:23"

I'm sorry, who are you and what did you do with my baby?

After I picked my jaw up off the ground, amazed that my three year old had now memorized more scripture than I had, I started to giggle. See, in his cute little three-year-old voice, when he recited the verse and line number, it sounded like he said, "Colossians free twenty free." It was absolutely adorable.

I can't really explain why that memory has stuck with me, but recently, I realized Jackson's words are more than just a cute mispronunciation. They actually hold a greater truth.

When we are working more for God and less for man, we gain a new freedom we may not have noticed before. When we choose to value God's opinion over everyone else's, we achieve a true sense of freedom—freedom from judgment, freedom from comparison, freedom from the pressure of being someone we're not.

I'll admit, at the time, I thought Colossians 3:23 was a strange verse to have children memorize. I was hoping for something more along the lines of "Honor your father and mother, as the Lord your God commanded you," (Deuteronomy 5:16) or "Children, obey your parents in the Lord, for this is right" (Ephesians 6:1). You know, something to make my mom life a little easier.

Over the last seven years, though, I've come to see the wisdom of those words from Colossians. As it turns out, it's a verse I need to repeat to myself every single day. I still get caught up worrying about what others think and striving for tangible rewards. This verse keeps me grounded and helps me remember who I am and whose I am.

What is holding you hostage? I know for me, I often feel trapped by guilt and doubt, but there is good news. There's a way to break free. By shifting our focus and looking up, we are reminded of our greater purpose: If we work for the Lord, we are rewarded with the freedom to be who He wants us to be.

That's a lesson I hope we never forget.

Under His Wings

He will cover you with his feathers, and under his wings you will find refuge; his faithfulness will be your shield and rampart.

Psalm 91:4

I hate hugs.

Ok, wait, that's not entirely true. I'm just not always fond of hugs I don't initiate. I guess I'm kinda like Vivian in *Pretty Woman*—"I say who. I say when."

One of my friends in college was bound a determined to break me of my hug-free habit. She would intentionally come up and hug me in the Dining Hall and just squeeze the heck out of me for an unusually long period of time. I think it was her version of exposure therapy. The whole time she was hugging me, she would be whispering, "It's going to be ok. Just accept it and relax." While I eventually became used to her shenanigans, I never could quite settle into the hug.

It's funny how life works out because I ended up marrying the world's best hugger. Even this self-proclaimed hug-avoider can confess Alex has the perfect amount of squeeze. He's spent the last 10 years training the boys in his art of hugging, and I have ended up squished in the middle of a four-man hugfest on more than one occasion. Their giggles do make the hugs a little more bearable.

I realized what a good hugger Alex is a few summers ago when I was isolated in Rock Hill for two weeks taking care of my mom when she had Covid. Those days were full of anxiety, as I worried about why she wasn't getting better, how the boys were doing in Columbia, and what school would look like in the fall. Exhausted and anxious, that was a time in my life when I truly craved a hug.

Sometimes, though, I wonder if it's not so much about the hug itself but about the sense of calm that comes with it. Even when I don't really want a hug, Alex knows when I need one, and I have to admit, they do make me feel better after a rough day. My troubles seem to melt away, if only for a minute. Maybe the science is right and hugs really do lower stress.

Unfortunately for you, I can't have Alex walking around giving out a bunch of free hugs (#awkward), but I can recommend another source of comfort and peace. Psalm 91:4 tells us, *He will cover you with His feathers, and under His wings you may seek refuge; His faithfulness is a shield and bulwark.* Like a mother bird, God offers us protection and a safe place to land during life's storms.

I don't know what you're going through right now, but I know God's got you. We all face challenges in life, some big, some small. Through them all, we can rest in God, knowing He is there to comfort us at the end of a long day. He wants to wrap His arms around us and whisper words of encouragement to each of us.

All we have to do is lean in and let Him.

What's Important

Give generously to them and do so without a grudging heart; then because of this the LORD *your God will bless you in all your work and in everything you put your hand to.*

Deuteronomy 15:10

You know what's weird about being a parent? Sometimes when I'm giving the boys advice and teaching them something, I realize I need the words just as much as they do.

Case in point . . .

Reeves had a hard time completing his work at school this week, so much so, his teacher emailed me Tuesday and Wednesday with her concerns. So Wednesday night, Reeves and I had a heart to heart, and somewhere along the way, I said, "School is the most important thing," to which Reeves responded, "More important than God and family?"

Of course, the answer was *no*, but at the same time, I needed Reeves to know I meant business about getting his ducks in a row.

Now, I don't know where you do your best thinking, but I do mine in the shower, so it wasn't until Thursday morning that I had my epiphany and figured out what I was really trying to say. I didn't mean school was the most important thing. I meant Reeves' *effort* at school was what was important. Because here's the thing about effort—it transcends school. It's a trait that shows up in sports, in work, in relationships, in life. And knowing the value of effort was what I wanted to emphasize.

I shared my thinking with Reeves before school and explained that effort was what I was looking for. He didn't need to get all of his work right, he just needed to show he was trying. That's what was important.

Naturally, he looked at me and quipped, "Even more important than God?"

This time I was ready with my reply: "No, but God has given us all talents and gifts, and He expects us to put forth some effort in using them. He doesn't need us to be perfect, but he does need us to try."

Yeah, buddy, I dropped the mic on that one! I was pretty proud of myself . . . until I started wondering if I were following my own advice.

On my way to school, I kept thinking about the story of Elijah and the widow in I Kings 17. The widow uses the little bit of oil and flour she has to make bread for Elijah, and because she does, God continues to bless her so that she never runs out of ingredients. She was afraid she didn't have enough, but she offered what she had, and God took it from there. She made the effort; God made the miracle.

That's usually how it works, if we're willing to try.

So, is there a talent or gift you've been holding back because you're worried it's not enough? I get it; I find myself doing the same thing. But let's make a pact, right here, right now, to give God our best effort and then watch what He will do.

I have a feeling we'll be pleasantly surprised by the results.

Press Pause

Therefore do not worry about tomorrow, for tomorrow will worry about itself. Each day has enough trouble of its own.

Matthew 6:34

My first married Christmas was miserable.

Being young and naïve, Alex and I thought we could please everybody, so we woke up in Rock Hill to celebrate with my mom, drove to Lexington for lunch at his mom's, and then trekked to his dad's for dinner and gifts. By the end of the day, we were less Clark Griswold and more Ebenezer Scrooge. Truthfully, we were living our own version of *Four Christmases* without the benefit of Vince Vaughn's jokes to lighten the mood.

The problem with the whole thing wasn't that I was exhausted by the end of the day. I mean, that was pre-kids, when I didn't need a daily nap and three cups of coffee. The problem was Alex and I couldn't enjoy being at one house because we were anxiously planning our departure and worrying about getting to the next house on time.

As we've gotten older, Alex and I have gotten much better at making plans that allow us to enjoy each celebration without the pressure of getting to the next family, but it recently occurred to me, we might not be passing that know-how down to our boys.

Jackson is my mini-me, meaning he is all about a schedule. What can I say—I live my life by a bell. But when we were in Atlanta over Spring Break, I realized this characteristic isn't necessarily one I want to pass on.

Before we left for Atlanta, Jackson made an itinerary with our daily destinations, which was fun because it got us all excited about the trip. When we got to Atlanta, though, I noticed his schedule was starting to steal his joy. At the Georgia Aquarium, he kept asking about the upcoming Braves game; when we were at the Braves game, he kept checking my phone to see if we'd have time to go to the zoo after the game or if we'd need to save that for the next day; and when we were at the World of Coke, he kept looking at my weather app to be sure our trip to the zoo wouldn't be rained out.

After about the third time he asked for my phone, I turned to him and said, "Can you calm down about later and just enjoy where we are now?"

I immediately felt guilty saying that because I understood exactly where he was coming from. He finds comfort in the security of knowing what's next, and that's totally normal. I feel the same way a lot of times myself. But even though I understood his thinking, I didn't want him to miss out on where we were by worrying too much about what was to come.

I read a quote a few years ago on a friend's blog that said, "Be where your feet are," and it's stuck with me. Unfortunately, that idea is easier said than done, especially in a culture of FOMO. It's easy to get caught up thinking about what we're missing or what's coming later, but what if what we're missing out on isn't an event happening elsewhere? What if what we're missing out on is the experience happening right in front of us because we're too busy planning ahead to notice it? Maybe that's what we should fear.

When my brain starts getting ahead of itself and I lose sight of the here and now, I try to remember this verse from The Message version of Ecclesiastes 5:18-20: *God deals out joy in the present, the now.* I don't know about you, but I like some joy in my life, making this verse a good reminder to stay focused on today.

Living life isn't like watching a movie. We lose out on the magic of the moment when we try to fast forward. And since we don't have the luxury of being able to rewind our lives, we can't go back to relive a missed experience. Once it's gone, it's gone.

So, let's all take a minute this week to press pause, to find joy in the present, and to soak in the now, knowing tomorrow will take care of itself.

And In This Corner...

Therefore encourage one another and build each other up, just as in fact you are doing.

I Thessalonians 5:11

There's an old joke that goes something like this:

The word of the day is *catacomb*. I will now prepare to use it in a sentence: Don King's hair is so crazy, somebody needs to get that cat a comb.

Hey, I said it was an old joke; I never said it was good one!

In case you've never heard of Don King or his famous hair, he is a prominent boxing promoter, most famous for publicizing Muhammad Ali's *Rumble in the Jungle* with George Foreman and his *Thrilla in Manila* with Joe Frazier. Known for being brash and outspoken, King's job as a promoter was to get fans pumped about upcoming fights by touting his boxer's skill and telling anybody who would listen how great the boxer was.

The older I get, the more I realize we could all use our own personal version of Don King—albeit maybe one who's a little less shady than the original.

We all need a promoter, someone who believes in us 100 percent, who tells other people how great we are, even when, or maybe especially when, we can't see greatness in ourselves. Someone who will bet it all on us and who will talk junk to the haters on our behalf.

I'll be honest, it's taken me awhile to get here. In my younger years, I was deluded enough to think that if I pointed out someone else's strengths, I was somehow taking away from myself. Truthfully, I guess I wasn't deluded as much as I was insecure. But that idea simply isn't true.

It's funny how turning 40 can change things, and I don't just mean my new reliance on readers and face cream. This decade has changed my perspective and has given me a security in my own skin I didn't have before. Now I can see that shining a light on someone else's talents doesn't diminish my own. Lifting someone else up doesn't mean I'm putting myself down. In fact, the opposite is true. Iron sharpens iron (Proverbs 27:17), and I know that surrounding myself with my squad of rock stars just makes me better. I'm so proud of them for fighting for important causes, leading influential organizations, loving on their families and friends, and sharing their gifts with others. They motivate me more than they know.

The world is full of naysayers, voices that say we can't or we shouldn't. Voices that say we're too young, too old, too slow, too weak, too late, too weird, too different.

Let this be a challenge to be the voice that pushes through the negativity and cheers for the good. Be the voice that says someone else is so funny, so talented, so kind, so creative, so courageous. In other words, let's follow the command of I Thessalonians 5:11 and "build each other up and encourage one another."

I'm thankful to be blessed with so many Don Kings who build me up each and every day, who see things in me I don't always see in myself, and who encourage me to follow my dreams. My goal is to return the favor.

So, if your friend has a business, rep her swag. If your friend gets a promotion, take her out and toast her success. And if your friend is having a bad hair day, give that cat a comb and tell her she looks awesome.

After all, we only have one life to live, and it's way more fun when we do it celebrating each other.

Grabbing Grace

But now that you have been set free from sin and have become slaves of God, the benefit you reap leads to holiness, and the result is eternal life. For the wages of sin is death, but the gift of God is eternal life in Christ Jesus our Lord.

Romans 6:22-23

If you don't know my son Jackson, you wouldn't know his all-time favorite food is tacos. I mean, the boy got a tortilla blanket and his very own taco holders for his ninth birthday.

And if you don't know Jackson, you'd also never know that his addiction to tacos is followed closely by an obsession with claw machines. That's right, the ridiculously rigged game that leaves children all around the world heartbroken and penniless is my son's passion. Oddly enough, he's weirdly good at it.

Knowing Jackson's two loves, it comes as no surprise that his favorite restaurant in Columbia is Casa Linda, our local Mexican restaurant, where he can indulge in his need for tacos and his zeal for the claw. I admit, it's not the worst way to blow two dollars, since he usually shares his prizes with his brothers.

What we only recently discovered is that Jackson can play the claw game from the comfort of our very own home, thanks to an app called Clawee. Granted, we miss out on queso and margaritas at Casa Linda, but that seems a small price to pay for 24/7 claw access.

Jackson and I are the early risers in our house. This week, I was dozing on the couch while he checked MLB scores on my phone. In my sleepy haze, I heard him casually mention he was going to try out Clawee. After a few minutes of blissful silence, I was jarred awake by an exclamation of "I won!" followed by words that sent shivers down my spine: "Mom, do I press the 'ship now' button?"

"NOOOOOOOOO!!!!"

I sprang off the couch like it was on fire and quickly scrambled to delete the app before Jackson could have a truck load of toy Pikachus delivered to our house, courtesy of my Apple Pay. In his defense, he did claim he would save them for Reeves' birthday.

Throughout all of the chaos, Jackson kept insisting, "But, Mom, it's free."

Bless his sweet, innocent heart.

I tried to explain that the Pikachu wasn't really free. At some point, somebody was going to have to pay for something, and since that somebody was most likely going to be me, I had to draw the line before he maxed out my credit card buying stuffed animals. (I should note, that's actually a true genetic possibility, seeing as how I did that exact thing once buying Beanie Babies in college, and no, I truly cannot explain how things got so out of hand.)

Anyway, maybe because this happened Monday morning and Easter was on my mind from church the day before, I said something like, "Nothing in this world is free, Jack . . . well, nothing except God's love, and Jesus actually paid a price for that, but it's free to us." Evidently, 6 a.m. isn't the best time to have a theological conversation with a nine year old. Jackson promptly hopped off the couch to wake up Reeves and tell him how mean his mom is and how she wouldn't let his loving brother win him a mailbox full of "free" Pikachus. Thanks, Jack.

After triple checking that Clawee was, in fact, deleted, I fixed a cup of coffee and opened my journal, where I came face to face with my verse of the day, Romans 6:23: *For the wages of sin is death, but the free gift of God is eternal life in Christ Jesus our Lord.* I always say God is the original Alexa with the ability to make scriptures appear minutes after I talk about them. When God sends me the same memo in multiple ways, it's cool; when Alexa sends me ads, it's just plain creepy.

This message was loud and clear—the gift of God's everlasting love is free to us without price. God isn't playing any sort of game with us, and He hasn't rigged the outcome so that we end up empty handed. If we let God into our hearts, we win the incredible blessings He has for us, including eternal life. God longs to drop His gifts into our hands, we just have to open them and be willing to receive everything He has in store for us.

When we celebrate Easter, and throughout the rest of the year too, let's focus on the real prize we've won: God sent his one and only son to die for our sins. May we receive this offering of His love with open hands, thankful for His sacrifice and His grace, and may we strive to share His love with others each and every day.

Can You Hear Me Now?

People of Zion, who live in Jerusalem, you will weep no more. How gracious he will be when you cry for help! As soon as he hears, he will answer you. Although the Lord gives you the bread of adversity and the water of affliction, your teachers will be hidden no more; with your own eyes you will see them. Whether you turn to the right or to the left, your ears will hear a voice behind you, saying, "This is the way; walk in it."

Isaiah 30:19-21

Growing up, I was a really shy student who never liked asking questions. I was self-conscious about my voice, and I didn't want everybody to look at me. Now that I'm a teacher, I'm more confident and ask questions when I'm confused. I figure I'm probably not the only one with the question, and even if I am, that's okay, at least I'm participating. Teachers really like that.

So, when I was confused in Sunday school a few weeks ago, I assertively raised my hand and said, "This may be a dumb question, but what exactly is *sanctification*?"

One of my friends looked at me and said, "That's a dumb question." Or, at least that's what I thought he said. So, being the sweet girl I am, I promptly told him to shut up. (We really are a loving group, I promise!)

The problem was, he wasn't trying to bash me. What he actually said was, "There's no such thing as a dumb question." Dang! Poor guy was trying to make me feel better, and I ended up biting his head off simply because I misheard him.

Hearing has been a problem for me my whole life. When I was in elementary school, we were all sent to the school nurse, who administered a hearing test. I remember it vividly.

The nurse explained we would put on a set of headphones and listen for a high or low tone. Depending on which ear we heard it in, we would raise the corresponding hand. If you're a child of the '80s, you probably know exactly what I'm talking about.

When it was my turn, I put on those huge headphones that were so big and heavy, they made my little eight-year-old neck wobble, and I waited for the beep. I waited and I waited and I waited. After about a minute, the nurse took off the headphones and gently began to repeat the directions to me. When she finished, I looked at her and replied, "Yes, ma'am, I understand what I'm supposed to do, but I haven't heard a beep yet." Houston, we have a problem. As it turned out, I did have some hearing loss and had to make a few trips to the local speech and hearing clinic.

As you can imagine, hearing loss is a bit problematic for an English teacher who likes discussions. I often have to ask kids to repeat themselves, and I find myself saying, "You're not wrong, I just can't hear you," at least once a day.

I especially have trouble hearing low pitches, which makes it more difficult for me to hear and understand guys than girls. Pretty ironic, since I seem to hear all the guys in my house way better than they hear me.

But the voice I have the most trouble hearing is God's.

It's not that I don't know what to do to hear His voice. I know I should pray about things. I know I should read the Bible. I know I should find time to be quiet. It's just that sometimes I have a hard time discerning what God's telling me. Sometimes I can't figure out if I'm hearing God's true voice, or if I'm hearing what I want Him to say. I find myself thinking, "Is this really what God wants me to do, or is this me pretending my desires are His instructions?"

I truly believe this whole problem could be solved if God would just hook me up with the burning bush I keep asking for.

In the meantime, I have found one practice that helps me hear God's voice. Research has shown that immersion is one of the best ways to learn and understand a language, so over the past few years, that has been my strategy for learning God's language. By reading devotions, studying the Bible, listening to sermons, singing songs, and talking with trusted friends, I have tried to give myself more opportunities to hear His voice and feel His nudges.

One of the best examples of this strategy working happened the summer of 2018. In July, I wrote a blog post for Columbia Moms Blog about my doubts and fears about expanding our family. I was leaving the AP Summer Institute in Charlotte the morning it posted, and as I was walking to my car to head back to Columbia, I got a text from a close friend who had read the post. As a new mom of three herself, she encouraged me that I could handle it and suggested I listen to Zach Williams' song *Fear Is a Liar*. I read the text as I was getting in the car, and when I cranked it up, that exact song was just coming on the radio. I was so stunned, I couldn't even back out of my parking space. It was a moment when I knew God was talking directly to me, telling me not to be afraid, assuring me that He was with me.

When I was little, one of my favorite shows was *The Dukes of Hazzard*, which is where I learned the phrase, "Got your ears on?" It's CB radio speak to make sure the person you want to talk to is listening. These days, I say it to the boys when I really want them to pay close attention. It's funny because they'll say, "Yes, ma'am," and then hesitantly touch their ears just to be sure they're still there.

None of us will probably ever have a burning bush, but that doesn't mean we can't hear God's voice. God can use words, music, and people to transmit His messages to us. We just have to tune in to the right frequency and have our ears on, ready to listen.

Floating on Faith

Now faith is confidence in what we hope for and assurance about what we do not see.

Hebrews 11:1

Did you know a search on Amazon for "parenting books" will yield over 60,000 results? These books will come from a wide variety of experts, like Dr. Spock, John Rosemond, and the American Academy of Pediatrics, and they will have a wide variety of titles, everything from *Parenting with Love and Logic* to *Duct Tape Parenting*. (I have to admit, I'm dying to read that one!)

The majority of these books seem like they offer good advice and would be good places to turn with parenting questions. But you know where I'm not looking for parenting advice?

The Old Testament.

Think about it. There's the story of a mom who convinces her son to take advantage of his dad's failing eyesight and steal his brother's birthright. Then there's the story of a dad who favors one son so much, his brothers end up hating him and selling him into slavery. If you ask me, these people aren't making the cover of *Parents* magazine anytime soon.

But the one that really gets me is the story about the mom who puts her baby in a basket and floats him down a river. Not only was this river notorious for crocodiles, but I'm pretty sure that basket didn't come with a 5-point safety harness.

When I hear the story of baby Moses, I'm often overcome with the same incredulousness Reese Witherspoon has in

Sweet Home Alabama when she looks at her friend and says, "Look at you, you have a baby . . . in a bar." She knows what she is seeing is totally inappropriate. And I feel the same way toward Moses' mom—"Look at you, you put a baby . . . in a basket." It's like, "Ma'am, what made you think that was a good idea?"

But after almost 3,650 days of this mom gig, I'm starting to understand where Jochebed was coming from.

There's no doubt in my mind that Moses' mom loved him with all of her heart. She wanted what was best for him, and she was ready to do everything in her power to protect him, even if it meant hiding him in reeds along the bank of the Nile.

I can't imagine the fear she must have felt, knowing her son's life was at stake, but I do understand the stress of trying to do the right thing when the outcome isn't exactly clear.

As parents, we often live in the land of uncertainty. My friends and I seem to be in a period of parenting where we're faced with some big questions every day. Questions like *Which school should we choose? Does she need a tutor? Should he see a psychologist? Should we hold her back?* These are big, important questions, none of which can be taken lightly.

It's so easy to overthink each situation and get caught up in the "what-ifs." But imagine if Jochebed had done that. If she had spent too much time going back and forth, debating the pros and cons of her options, Pharaoh's men would have been at her door, and Moses' fate would have been sealed. Ultimately, she had to make a choice and have faith in her plan. At some point, we, too, have to make the best decisions we can with the information we've been given and then let them float on down the river.

Most days, I feel like for every good parenting decision I make, I probably make two bad ones, but thankfully, there's good news. God works in every decision we make, the good ones and the bad. Even when I make a mistake, God can take my mess and turn it into a miracle. After all, being sold into slavery was what allowed Joseph to end up in the position to save his family from starvation.

Parenting is hard work, no doubt about it. As I continue to make decisions for the boys, my prayer is that my faith will overcome my fear, and like Jochebed, I'll take comfort in knowing God is steering my boat.

Just One of the Guys

For there is one God and one mediator between God and mankind, the man Christ Jesus, who gave himself as a ransom for all people.

I Timothy 2:5-6

I love my boys, I really do, but sometimes, they try my patience, what with their constant wrestling and silly name calling. A few Sundays ago, after the fifth, "You're a poopy head," I just snapped. Maybe because it was Sunday and we had just gotten home from church, or maybe because nothing else seemed to be working, I looked at them and said, "Excuse me, but do you think Jesus talked to his brother like that?"

The boys stopped, looked at me with puppy dog eyes, and very solemnly said, "No, ma'am." My strategy worked . . . they didn't even start wrestling again until I left the room.

As I walked away, I had to laugh because honestly, Jesus may have talked to James *exactly* like that. After all, Jesus was fully human, something I learned the hard way back in 1995 when I was a senior in high school.

I remember the Sunday school lesson like it was yesterday. Our teacher had given us a Christmas quiz, and since he was a dad of toddlers, we were playing for Cheerios. Now, normally, I'm not a big fan of Cheerios, I'm more of a Froot Loop kinda girl, but I am a big fan of winning in general, so the prize didn't really matter. I was in it to win it.

It all came down to the last question. I was tied for the lead with a guy who was normally one of my good friends, but that day, the gloves were off.

The last question was "What did baby Jesus do when he was born?" I chose the answer that basically said the baby awakes but no crying he makes.

I remember thinking, quite smugly I'll admit, that I had the game in the bag, so imagine my complete and utter shock when I lost.

See, I didn't choose the right answer. I chose the words to a Christmas carol. But my friend, he chose the right answer. He chose the answer that said Jesus cried just like every baby does.

The idea that Jesus was a regular little baby who cried like every other newborn was a new concept to me that day, but it is a truth that has stuck with me ever since.

Fast forward to 2007. Our first Christmas together, I took Alex home to Rock Hill, and my mom asked him to say the blessing. Talk about being thrown straight into the hot seat!

I have no idea what Alex said during the blessing, but I do remember how he ended it. Instead of a simple, "Amen," Alex said, "Bye, God."

If you've been here long enough, you know exactly what happened when I heard that . . . I died laughing at the dining room table. I mean, who says that? "Bye, God!" just seemed a little too casual, a little too personal. I was trying (unsuccessfully) to stifle my laughter when my mom looked at me and snapped, "Stop laughing. That's exactly the kind of relationship you should have with God."

You know what they say . . . Mothers know best.

I often think of God and Jesus as these faraway beings, out of touch with our daily lives, but they're not. It's no coincidence that when God sent his son to the world on Christmas, He called him Emmanuel, *God with us*. At the dining room table, on Sunday mornings, in our relationships, God is with us.

It's easy to forget that Jesus was human too. He gets us. He knows what it's like to lose loved ones. He knows what it's like to feel judged. And he probably even knows what it's like to have a pesky brother driving him crazy every now and then.

And because Jesus gets us, we can be real with God. We don't have to hide our thoughts, not that we really could anyway. We don't have to feel ashamed or embarrassed or unworthy. Because He came as a baby, we can talk to Him as a friend.

So, wherever you are today, know that God is always with you, ready to listen like the most trusted and loving of friends. He doesn't care what you say or how you say it, just that you share what's on your heart.

That's always the right answer.

I Like Big Buts

"I have told you these things, so that in me you may have peace. In this world you will have trouble. But take heart! I have overcome the world."

John 16:33

One year, over Thanksgiving break, when I was able to enjoy the boys' constant company for five days in a row, I noticed something . . . my house is full of buts. And I'm not just saying that because the guys in my house love to run around in their Avengers underwear. No, I mean my house is full of "buts," one t, not two. The conjunction, not the body part.

What I noticed over Thanksgiving was that every time I said something to the boys, it was met with a **but**.

But, Mom, he started it.

But, Mom, I'm not tired.

But, Mom, I don't want the 3-course meal you spent all day cooking; I want a PB&J.

The whole situation reminded me of the episode of *How I Met Your Mother* when Ted's students notice that during her news show, Robin has a tendency to say, "But, umm." She says it so much, they create a drinking game around her show, taking a drink every time she says, "But, umm," which, sadly for her, turned out to be quite often. I have to admit, by the end of day three with the boys, I was ready to come up with a "But, Mom!" game of my very own.

To be honest, the boys were driving me nuts with all of their buts, until I had a disturbing epiphany. What if their use of the word **but** was learned behavior?

Let's face it, I can be just as guilty of using that word as they are.

I need to clean the house, but I think I'll read a book instead.

I should wake up and work out, but my bed is so warm.

I should cook a healthy dinner, but Chic-fil-a is so much easier.

In essence, I use **but** to make excuses that allow me to do what I want to do. Nowhere in my life is this more evident than in my reluctance to follow God's will.

I need to get up early and have my quiet time, but I'm too tired.

I should probably invite so-and-so to church, but she might think I'm weird.

I should be more vocal about my faith, but people may judge me

Maybe the boys use **but** so much because they hear me rely on it every day to stay in my comfort zone.

The good news is, **but** doesn't have to be a bad word. A few years ago, a friend shared a powerful way to use it. When she feels anxious, nervous, or totally ill-equipped to do something, she follows her doubt with "But God." It looks something like this:

I don't know how this is going to work out, but God does.

I don't think I can do this, but God can.

I'm too scared to make a change, but God is with me.

Life is full of uncertainty. It's full of tough decisions, challenging relationships, and leaps of faith. The key is to remember the biggest **but** of them all:

I have told you these things, so that in me you may have peace. In this world you will have trouble. ***BUT*** *take heart! I have overcome the world* (John 16:33, emphasis added).

As we go through our daily lives, may we remember we don't have to live in fear. We don't have to make excuses. And we don't have to go it alone. Instead, may we abide in the hope, the peace, the joy, and the love the greatest gift brings.

Trusting What We Can't See

For I know the plans I have for you," declares the LORD, *"plans to prosper you and not to harm you, plans to give you hope and a future.*

Jeremiah 29:11

I've never been much for New Year's resolutions, mainly because I can't keep them going. No matter how many times I've tried, I can't seem to make myself wash my face at night, run five miles a week, or bring all of my coffee cups in from the car for more than a few days after January 1.

A few years ago, a friend introduced me to the concept of choosing a word to focus on throughout the year instead of making a resolution, and I'm happy to say, this practice has been much more doable.

Several years ago, after a great deal of thought, I decided on the word **trust**. Not only did I choose it as my word, but I also drank the Kool-Aid and ordered one of those My Intent bracelets with my word engraved on it. I figured this would serve as a daily reminder to focus on my word and put it into practice.

Easier said than done.

I was feeling pretty good about my choice until I heard one of my friends had chosen the word **execute**, and as soon as I heard it, I wished I had picked it instead. **Execute** is such a strong, powerful word. It makes me feel like I'm kicking butt and taking names. I'm making things happen. And even better, I can see the action taking place. It's the sense of accomplishment and satisfaction I have when I make a to-do list and then mark things off one by one.

I think maybe that's why I'm having a hard time with trust. It doesn't always lead to immediate, easy-to-see results that help me stay focused, so I'm finding I have to have a great deal of patience. Sometimes I think I'm trusting, but am I really? It's easy to stop trusting without even realizing it.

Let's be honest, though, the real issue I have with trust is that it requires me to relinquish some, if not all, of my control. Whether it's in relationships with friends and family, or with God himself, trust forces me to rely on someone else, and that can be pretty scary.

A few days ago, I woke up early for my quiet time, knowing I had four big things I really wanted to pray about. I felt confident that I had done what I could do and was ready to leave the rest up to God. But by 4:30 that afternoon, my trust was really beginning to waver because I felt like I was only 1 for 4 in getting the answers I was hoping for.

Later that night, I was cleaning the boys' bathroom and thinking about my prayers that didn't get answered the way I wanted them to, when all of a sudden, I heard a voice. Now, I would like to be able to stop right here and tell you I heard God's voice speaking to me plain as day, and it sounded a lot like James Earl Jones, but alas, that's not quite how this story goes.

The voice I heard was actually none other than Ricky Ricardo's, complete with his thick Cuban accent. If you've ever watched *I Love Lucy*, you know at least once an episode, Lucy got into a little trouble, causing Ricky to exclaim, "Lucy! You got some 'splainin' to do."

And so, as I scrubbed the tub, questioning why things went the way they did and how everything could possibly work out, I could hear myself in Ricky's voice telling God he had some 'splainin' to do of his own.

And then I had to stop and laugh at myself because who am I to tell God he needs to explain himself to me? I'm pretty sure most days I need to explain myself to Him, clarifying why I did what I did, or even harder, why I didn't do what I needed to.

One of my good friends says God's plan is like a puzzle—we only get to see one little piece at a time, but He can see what the entire finished puzzle looks like. I like that image, and sometimes, when I'm hesitant to put my trust in something I can't see, focusing on that image of a puzzle keeps me grounded and makes things more concrete. It reminds me that there's more to this one particular answer, this one particular event, this one particular day than I can even imagine.

Most days, I feel pretty good about praying; where I struggle is in putting my complete and total trust in God. In trusting His plan to be way better than my own. In trusting that He will answer my prayers, in His time and in His way.

Because as easy as it was to engrave the word *trust* on a bracelet, I'm still working day by day to engrave it on my heart.

Famous Last Words

The right word spoken at the right time is as beautiful as gold apples in a silver bowl.

Proverbs 25:11

Peace and quiet is hard to come by in a house full of rough and tumble boys, so I take the "me time" I do get very seriously.

One Sunday, I was sitting at the kitchen table, sipping my coffee and enjoying three blissful minutes of quiet when Jackson came bounding in, asking what he could have for breakfast. Frustrated that my moment of silence had been interrupted, I offhandedly said, "Whatever you can find."

Famous.Last.Words.

Jackson looked at me with a twinkle in his eyes, promptly grabbed a bag of leftover soccer snack Oreos off the table, and dissolved into a fit of delighted giggles.

"Jackson! No! You can't have Oreos for breakfast!"

He looked me dead in the eyes and said, "You said 'whatever you can find.' You have to be careful with your words, Mom."

Then he scurried back to the den, no doubt to gloat over his breakfast of champions, never realizing how true his words were.

Because Jackson's exactly right—we do have to be careful with our words, as they have the power to hurt and to heal. Thankfully, we have the opportunity to use our words for good every single day. Proverbs 16:24 tells us *Gracious words are a honeycomb, sweet to the soul and healing to the bones.*

The good news is it takes absolutely no money and not much time to be nice. It could be the friendly greeting offered to the Target cashier, an encouraging text to a friend, a verbal high five for a job well done, or a compliment on a social media post. We never know when our words will be the sweet spot in someone's day.

One of my oldest friends avoided Oreos in high school because, as she said, "A moment on the lips, a lifetime on the hips."

I think the same can be said about the power of gracious words—it only takes a moment to offer them, but their impact can last a lifetime.

Shadrach, Meshach, and A Here We Go

"If we are thrown into the blazing furnace, the God we serve is able to deliver us from it, and he will deliver us from Your Majesty's hand. But even if he does not, we want you to know, Your Majesty, that we will not serve your gods or worship the image of gold you have set up."

Daniel 3:17-18

One of my best friends from college briefly dated a guy named Shad. Naturally, our friend group delighted in asking her if Meshach and Abednego would be joining in on the date, or if she were "fired up" for the evening. You know, all the loving and supportive questions you ask a friend as she embarks on a new relationship.

As it turned out, Shad didn't quite live up to his namesake and was only in the picture for a few months. But Shadrach, Meshach, and Abednego? Those guys are legendary. You see, these three friends are well-known for coming out of King Nebuchadnezzar's furnace completely untouched, but that's not actually the coolest thing they did.

What sets them apart to me is the fact that they went into the fiery furnace to begin with.

The truly amazing part of their story is that Shadrach, Meshach, and Abednego entered the furnace without hesitating, without second-guessing their decision, and without looking back. They had swagger. They jumped in head first, telling Nebuchadnezzar, "If we are thrown into the blazing furnace, the God we serve is able to deliver us from it, and he will deliver us from Your Majesty's hand. But even if he does not, we want you to know, Your Majesty, that we will not serve your gods or worship the image of gold you have set up" (Daniel 3:17-18). Talk about bold faith.

Now, I don't know about you, but I like a little more certainty in my life. Had I been with Shadrach, Meshach, and Abednego, I would have liked to have caught a glimpse of the angel waiting in the furnace *before* I stepped on in with such a brazen, no-nonsense attitude. But that's the thing about life, the only thing certain about it is that it's filled with uncertainty.

We all have our own versions of the fiery furnace, situations we're stepping into a little blind, unsure of the outcome. It could be taking a new job, moving to a new city, or fostering a child. For me, it was deciding to write this book. I really don't know if one person will read it or 100, but I knew I wanted to try, and I figured if those three guys could face the flames without flinching, surely I could publish a few of my own thoughts on the matter.

Our next steps aren't always going to be obvious. Entering the furnace isn't like driving into the carwash. There's no green light to tell us to enter, no flashing light to back up, and no red light to tell us to stop in this spot for maximum results. Life isn't always filled with clear, easy-to-read signs and signals, assuring us we're always making the right choices.

What is certain, though, is that God will be with us, walking with us every step of the way. He wants us to put our faith in Him completely, believing He will protect us without hesitation. It is as true today as it was when Moses spoke these words to Joshua: *The Lord himself goes before you and will be with you, he will never leave you nor forsake you. Do not be afraid; do not be discouraged* (Deuteronomy 31:8).

That's a legendary truth we can all get fired up about.

Opposites Attract

Do nothing out of selfish ambition or vain conceit. Rather, in humility value others above yourselves, not looking to your own interests but each of you to the interests of the others.

Philippians 2:3-4

Growing up in Rock Hill, my friends and I spent a good deal of time right up the road at Carowinds, an amusement park on the South Carolina-North Carolina border. I had friends who had season passes to Carowinds. I had friends who worked at Carowinds. And I even had a friend or two who got banned from Carowinds.

Carowinds is known for its exciting rides, as well as its special events, but there was one other reason my friends and I thought it was so great . . . the recording studio. For a small fee, we could finally cut the demo that was going to bring us fame and fortune. And we knew just which song to record—a cover of Paula Abdul's *Opposites Attract*.

Sadly, we never made it to the top of the charts with our version of the song, but it did make a lasting impression on me, mainly because the song speaks the truth.

Alex and I are definitely opposites. I like Clemson, he likes Carolina. I'm an early bird, he's a night owl. I majored in English, he majored in finance. I don't like for my food to touch, he mixes everything together (although I'm starting to think he does that just to freak me out). The list goes on and on.

But our biggest difference comes in our ability to talk to people, or in my case, my inability to do so.

Alex is an extrovert. He's a greeter, a hand shaker, and a hugger. He's comfortable in his own skin, and he gets energy from talking with others. This is what makes him a phenomenal salesman. The man could sell ice to an Eskimo.

I, on the other hand, struggled to sell Girl Scout cookies when I was little. I mean, y'all, that's bad. Those things pretty much sell themselves. But I'm an introvert, and the thought of talking to strangers, and sometimes even people I know, scares me and exhausts me all at once.

When we go to a social event, Alex jumps right in, while I like to hang back, hugging the wall and trying my best to be inconspicuous until I feel comfortable.

A few months ago, we were sitting in Sunday school waiting for the lesson to start, when Mr. John, the true backbone of our church, rolled in with the coffee cart. All of a sudden, from across the room, Alex yelled, "Hey, Mr. John!" waving to him like he was landing an airplane.

I scrunched down in my chair, thinking, "Calm down. You're so loud. Stop drawing attention to us." I just knew everybody was staring at us, thinking we were weirdos.

Once everything was set out, Alex got up to fix his coffee. That's when God sat right down beside me in Alex's empty chair, gave me the side eye, and said, "You know, Katherine, instead of thinking about how Alex's greeting made you feel, maybe you should think about how it made Mr. John feel."

Nothing like being put in your place by the Big Man himself.

I didn't have to think very hard about how Mr. John felt, it was written all over his face. He felt noticed, he felt appreciated, and he felt loved. Isn't that how we all want to feel?

I learned an important lesson that day: I can't control what people think about me, but I can control how I make other people feel.

Jesus went out of his way to make people feel welcomed. He talked to lepers, to sinners, to the lost, and to the least. And he really didn't care what other people thought about it.

I would love to say I no longer care what people think about me either, but that's simply not true. I'm a work in progress. Sometimes my fear still overtakes me. I revert to my shy side, and I don't reach out the way I know I should. But I'm trying to be better. To step out of my safety zone and truly treat other people the way I want to be treated: welcomed and included.

To be more like Jesus, sometimes we have to do the opposite of what feels comfortable. For me, that's making the first move and speaking to strangers, even though it makes me nervous. For you, it may be taking cookies to the new family down the street or talking to the homeless person at the grocery store or calling a friend to apologize.

It's not easy to be vulnerable, to do something that runs counter to our normal, even when we know it's the right thing to do. But let's agree to put ourselves out there . . . we may feel weird, but we may also make somebody feel loved.

And ultimately, that's what we are all called to do.

Herd Mentality

Just as a body, though one, has many parts, but all its many parts form one body, so it is with Christ. For we were all baptized by one Spirit so as to form one body whether Jews or Gentiles, slave or free—and we were all given the one Spirit to drink. Even so the body is not made up of one part but of many.

I Corinthians 12:12-14

A few years ago, I made a bucket list. It's not long, but it is rather unique, and it even includes riding a mechanical bull. At the top of my list is being a contestant on Jeopardy! I figure since I can be a regular contestant *or* a participant in the Teachers Tournament, I have really upped my odds of getting on the show. Plus, I already have one of my interesting anecdotes ready and waiting—I have been to the prom 16 times. Amazing, right? I feel sure Ken Jennings is dying to chat with me about that little tidbit.

I love everything about the prom . . . the dresses, the decorations, the awesome DJs that play four solid hours of music that makes me want to shake my groove thing.

Now, I know I said earlier I have been to 16 proms, but that's not exactly true. Technically, I have only been to 15 because I didn't quite make it to Prom 2012. Instead of going to the prom, I spent the evening in the hospital snuggling my sweet new baby boy.

The Friday morning of prom, I woke up bright and early, knowing that Jackson had not listened to my explicit instructions to stay right where he was until *after* Saturday night. The entire way to the hospital, I kept firing off texts to my co-sponsor Brea, detailing everything that needed to get done. Finally, Brea had had enough—it was 5 a.m. after all—

and sent me a text that basically said, "I got this. Stop texting me and go have a baby." Well, okay then.

Deep down, I knew Brea had it under control. She loves prom (and Jeopardy!) as much as I do, and she had a wonderful team of teachers and students backing her up. Pictures from the night proved that it was, indeed, a magical masquerade.

My problem that morning was I didn't want to have to ask for help. There I was in the middle of a contraction, too proud to admit I needed somebody else to take over setting up for a dance. If I hadn't been about to have his baby, I think Alex would have tossed me out of the car for such nonsense.

Why are we so afraid to ask for help? Is it that we don't want to appear weak? Is it that we are afraid of rejection if the person we're asking says no? Is it that we are afraid to release control—What if the person helping doesn't do it the same way we would have? Or worse, what if she does it better?

I feel like this is a human problem. I think the rest of the animal kingdom has it figured out.

If you know my boys, you know giraffes are a big deal in our house. Over the years, I've learned a lot about these animals, along with all the other animals that roam the African grasslands (Fingers crossed *African Animals* will be a Jeopardy! category). One thing sticks out about these animals—the majority of them live in herds, and the herds work together.

Take elephants, for example. While some members of the herd go out to find food, others stay behind to protect the young. Giraffes, especially, benefit from the herd. A giraffe is most vulnerable when it bends down to drink water, so while several giraffes drink, the other giraffes stay on the lookout for lions and other predators. In both cases, the animals survive because they help each other.

We should try to be more like giraffes. (Long legs? Yes, please!) It's taken almost 45 years, but I've finally figured out that—SHOCKER—I can't do it all by myself. And thankfully, I don't have to. Now, instead of being too prideful, embarrassed, or ashamed to ask for help, I count my blessings that I have family and friends to ask.

I read once that when we turn down help, we have taken away a friend's chance to serve, the chance for her to be the hands and feet of Jesus. I don't know about you, but that's not something I want to get in the way of. God made us part of a body of believers for a reason. He knew we would need each other, and He knows how much we can benefit from leaning on each other's gifts and talents. We are stronger together, no doubt about it.

In fact, I'd make it a true Daily Double and bet all my money on it.

You Can Go Your Own Way

Come to me, all you who are weary and burdened, and I will give you rest. Take my yoke upon you and learn from me, for I am gentle and humble in heart, and you will find rest for your souls. For my yoke is easy and my burden is light.

Matthew 11:28-30

If I could have any job in the world, I would absolutely be a singer/songwriter. It's not that I want the fame and the fans—although traveling across the country on a tricked out tour bus would be pretty cool—it's that I want to have that Zen moment all singer/songwriters seem to have when they are immersed in their music. When I think of singer/songwriters, I picture them at a mic, maybe standing with a guitar or sitting at a piano, singing their hearts out, eyes closed, faces turned upwards, just totally absorbed in the song and completely at peace in the moment.

Unfortunately, the good Lord didn't bless me with the ability to play the guitar or sing like Norah Jones. My college roommate, who was a talented Furman Singer herself, once told me what I lacked in talent, I made up for in enthusiasm. I think it was a compliment, maybe?

My friend Caroline is also a fan of singer/songwriters, most notably Stevie Nicks, which has led to her slight obsession with Fleetwood Mac. I love Caroline, but I gotta be honest, I don't really care that much about Fleetwood Mac. See, I'm an Eagles girl. What can I say, I guess I'm more of a *Desperado* than a *Gypsy*.

Recently, Caroline organized a group of ladies in our Sunday school class to read I and II Samuel during Advent.

You're probably wondering how those books connect to the Christmas story. Weeeeeell, they don't . . . at least not in the way that Old Testament books like Isaiah and Micah do. But they do contain plenty of examples of God fulfilling his promises, which is ultimately the heart and soul of Christmas.

Now, in case you're like I was and you're not quite up to date on the happenings of 1 Samuel 5 and 6, let me catch you up. The Philistines had just captured the Ark of the Covenant, only to realize wherever it was, the people in close proximity would be killed or afflicted with tumors. At first, the Philistines tried moving the Ark from city to city to see if that made a difference, but God continued to be heavy handed with the people. I guess He wasn't really in the mood to play hide and seek—he'd been there, done that in the Garden of Eden with Adam and Eve.

Finally, the Philistines had had enough of God's special attention and called it quits. They returned the Ark to the Israelites, along with parting gifts of golden rats and golden tumors, because who wouldn't want those?

On the morning we read 1 Samuel 5 and 6, Caroline sent all of us a text of her takeaways. She mentioned the Philistines sent the Ark of the Covenant back to the Israelites because, as she wisely pointed out, without the concrete reminder of God, the Philistines could "go their own way." Like I said, obsessed with Fleetwood Mac.

On my way to school, I kept singing that one line over and over, mainly because I don't know the rest of the song . . . fan of the Eagles, remember?

As I kept belting out, "You can go your own way, go your own waaaaaay," a question popped into my mind: Sure, you *can* go your own way, but why would you want to? I mean, we all have the ability to go our own ways, but that doesn't mean they are the right ways. Sometimes, my way leads to nothing but trouble, exhaustion, and stress, and who wants a bunch of that?

We can all go our own way, but God's way offers something different.

In Matthew 11:28-30, Jesus reminds us that God promises us rest if we hitch our yoke to his. When we go our own way, we become burdened and heavy laden, but when we go God's way, when we put our trust and hope in Him, even the most difficult paths become a little easier to travel. God's way provides a gentleness and a lightness that our ways don't.

One of my favorite worship songs is *Amazing Grace*, but not the original church hymnal version. Nope, I'm talking about the church camp-style one, you know, the one set to the tune of *Peaceful, Easy Feeling* by none other than the Eagles. *Amazing Grace* isn't my favorite because it's by the best band of the '70s, it's my favorite because I love the message. When we go God's way, we find the peaceful, easy feeling that comes with God's grace. Our fears diminish and are replaced by hope. Ultimately, when we take God's path, we can rest in His promises for each and every one of us.

When we write God's word on our hearts and face Him, we can feel His light shining on us in the darkest of times and experience the inner peace of His presence washing over us, just like one of those singer/songwriters I envision.

So, whether you're a gypsy or a desperado or someone in between, know there's always hope when we're standing on solid ground.

Lightening the Load

Bear one another's burdens, and so fulfill the law of Christ.

Galatians 6:2

One of my favorite quotes is by the Dalai Lama and says, "If you think you are too small to make a difference, try sleeping with a mosquito."

As a born and bred Southerner, this speaks to my heart, as I have suffered the wrath of those blood-sucking nuisances my entire life. I know the power they wield in their tiny, little bodies, and I rue Noah's decision to take two of them onto the ark way back when. What was he thinking?

But I digress. This story is not actually about my frustration with mosquitoes. This story is about the power of the small, seemingly insignificant tasks we undertake every day.

When my mom died, my friends immediately came to ease my burdens. They shared their housekeepers, they shopped for new church clothes for the boys, they organized an amazing celebration after the service, and they fed us meals for a good three months.

But out of all the things people did for me when my mom died, there's one that truly stands out: Two of my friends matched and folded all of my family's socks.

To understand the significance of this task, you first have to understand how many socks reside in the Bryant household. We have baseball socks, soccer socks, running socks, basketball socks (If someone could please explain to me why all these sports need different socks, I would greatly appreciate it!), dress socks, theme socks, crew socks, tall socks, tiny toddler socks . . . the list goes on and on. Imagine a laundry bag full of nothing but socks. That's how many socks we're talking.

Being the smart mamas that they are, they turned the chore into a party and got their kids in on the action. At one point, one of the girls stopped matching long enough to comment on our abnormally large number of socks and even questioned some of our (nonexistent) laundry practices. Not only did these friends match and fold all the socks, they brought them back to our house separated into plastic baggies labeled with each of our names. Talk about a labor of love.

The Bible is full of stories about big miracles that we know by heart, but sometimes the most important stories are the ones we don't pay much attention to.

Think about when Jesus sent two disciples to go pick up the donkey in Matthew 21. This task seems to be so insignificant—after all, we don't even know which two disciples Jesus sent—and yet it was, in actuality, a monumental task. Not only were the two disciples providing Jesus' mode of transportation into the most important week of His life, but they were also fulfilling a hundreds-year-old prophecy. I'm sure they thought they got stuck with the short end of the stick. Who really wants to lead a notoriously stubborn animal into town while probably having to scoop some poop along the way? They could never imagine the true magnitude of their job.

We don't always know the impact our seemingly small actions can have on the bigger picture. It could be holding the door open for a stranger, helping a friend out with carpool, or getting the oil changed for your spouse. We never know when an ordinary, everyday action can be just the thing to turn someone's day around and make them feel loved.

Every time I see a sock, which is often, because I think they multiply like Gremlins, I'm reminded of how blessed I am to have such wonderful friends. They made my burden lighter without even really realizing what they were doing.

Never underestimate the power of small gestures; sometimes they are what mean the most.

This Little Light of Mine

You are the light of the world. You cannot hide a city that is on a mountain. Men do not light a lamp and put it under a basket. They put it on a table so it gives light to all in the house. Let your light shine in front of men. Then they will see the good things you do and will honor your Father who is in heaven.

Matthew 5:14-16

Over my 22 years in the classroom, I have done a lot to boost school spirit. I've dressed up in a wide variety of costumes, from a deviled egg to Ralphie from *A Christmas Story*; I've danced the Dougie at a pep rally; I've been duct taped to the wall Statue of Liberty style; and I've even played in a faculty-student basketball game eight months pregnant. I may not always provide the most standards-based lessons, but when it comes to school spirit, I'm your girl. So when the administration recently asked for volunteers for the chicken wing eating contest, I didn't even have to think twice.

On the morning of the competition, the 7th grade guidance counselor and I went head to head on the morning news show with our cut downs and banter, so by the time of the contest that afternoon, the whole school was talking. To hear us tell it, this was going to be epic.

Long story short . . . I lost.

What can I say? I may be a champion trash talker, but I'm not exactly a champion wing eater.

After my tragic defeat in the first round, all of my students kept asking me what happened. How could I lose? I had been so confident.

Instead of trying to justify my loss or make excuses, I pointed out that my willingness to participate was what got them out of class. Amazing how quickly their ribbing turned into adoration.

See, I didn't have to win to be victorious. I won simply by showing up, and sometimes that's all we need to do.

A few years ago, a mentor shared something with me that changed the way I think about my role as a disciple.

She told me that our job isn't to change anybody's heart, only God can do that. Our job is to share our stories, to be open and honest about how God is working in our lives, to really just light the way. To be present in the darkness.

Man, I can't tell you what a relief it was to let go of the pressure that came with thinking I had to change someone's heart. It was freeing to shift my focus to shining my light for Him.

Now, I don't always get this right. Sometimes I still hesitate to share, I still ignore opportunities to reach out, and I still worry what others think. I am a work in progress, for sure. But I'm also noticing the older I get and the more I study the Bible, the more likely I am to recall Colossians 3:23 and take on the attitude of "You know what, bump it. I'm working for God, not for man, and if these people think I'm a little nutty, so be it."

My goal during the wing-eating contest wasn't to win it (LIE), my goal was to simply participate so that the event could take place and our students could have something fun to look forward to. It's the same with living out Matthew 5:14-16. We don't have to change anything, we just have to shine on the one who can change everything.

I have a poster in my classroom of the last few lines of *The Hill We Climb*, the poem Amanda Gorman recited at the 2020 Presidential Inauguration. The poem ends with these words: "For there is always light if only we're brave enough to see it, if only we're brave enough to be it."

Those words serve as my daily reminder to shine for the one who has blessed me in so many ways. May they be your reminder as well.

The Secret Is Out

For God so loved the world that he gave his one and only son, that whoever believes in him shall not perish but have eternal life.

John 3:16

I come from a long line of exceptionally good cooks. My grandmother, several of my great aunts, and my mom were all known for being queens of the kitchen.

I also come from a long line of shady cooks who were known for being super secretive with their recipes, even tweaking them a time or two before sharing.

Take, for example, the Legend of the Squash Casserole.

At some point in the '80s, my great aunt Margie, who was no slouch in the kitchen herself, sweet talked my grandmother into sharing her coveted squash casserole recipe, one that was rumored to be kept in a safety deposit box down at the Hartsville Bank and Trust.

A few weeks after sharing the recipe, Mimi casually asked Margie how the casserole turned out. Margie commented that it was good, if a little bit dry.

Mimi's innocent response: "How could it be dry with a cup of sour cream?"

In a state of shock, and a bit of outrage, Margie sputtered, "But, Margaret, you didn't tell me it had a cup of sour cream."

To which my grandmother coyly replied, "Oh, didn't I?"

The word *diabolical* comes to mind.

Now, I don't know if Mimi intentionally sabotaged the squash recipe or if that's just the stuff of family lore, but I do know there is a family recipe no one has shared for years . . . our recipe for trash.

You may be thinking to yourself, "Well, Katherine, who in their right mind would even want a recipe for trash? That sounds disgusting."

What I should clarify before you worry too much about our Stuckey-Smith culinary habits is that "trash" is what my family calls Chex mix. Always has, always will. Please don't try to change our ways.

Trash has been such a treat for our family and friends over the years, I made a batch to serve at my mom's funeral reception. It was a big hit, and the funeral director loved it so much, he asked for the recipe. I thought it would probably be ok to share it with one person who had done so much for us, but low and behold, when I went to look for it, the recipe had vanished. I couldn't find it anywhere, which was crazy since I had *just* used it.

I was heartbroken wondering how I was ever going to be able to keep our Christmas trash tradition alive. None of the recipes on the internet was quite right.

Then I remembered Mom had actually shared the recipe with her dear neighbor of 30 years, Lynn. Of all people, Lynn definitely deserved to be in on the secret. I mean, I love my mom, but she was the definition of high maintenance, so living next door to her wasn't always a bed of roses.

As it turned out, a friend in Rock Hill had recently asked Lynn for the recipe, and when she went to look for hers, it was missing too! Lynn and I got a real kick out of this turn of events. Even from the grave, Queenie was making darn sure nobody was getting their hands on *her* recipe.

While I can't share our trash recipe for fear of ghostly retribution, not to mention the fact that I can't actually find the dang thing, there is something the women in my family taught me that I can share, and that's how much God loves each and every one of us.

God's love for us is no secret. In fact, John 3:16 makes God's love for us plain as day: *For God so loved the world that he gave his one and only son, that whoever believes in him shall not perish but have eternal life.*

God's promise is straightforward. God doesn't keep His love locked away in a safety deposit box, and He doesn't make us jump through hoops to figure out any secret ingredients. There aren't any tricky techniques to master or tools to use. Jesus made the directions really simple in John 14:6: *I am the way and the truth and the life. No one comes to the Father except through me.*

So, that's it. The secret is out and ready to be shared. It all boils down to this: God offers his love to each of us without price. He wants us to be part of the family of believers, all we have to do is let Him into our lives.

Once we do that, He can whip up a masterpiece in each and every one of us.

Because My Mama Said So

Where can I go from your Spirit? Where can I flee from your presence? If I go up to the heavens, you are there; if I make my bed in the depths, you are there. If I rise on the wings of the dawn, if I settle on the far side of the sea, even there your hand will guide me, your right hand will hold me fast.

Psalm 139:7-10

We lost my mom in August.

I mean, we lost her, but the hospital like *lost* her, lost her. As in the man from the funeral home showed up to get her, and the hospital staff didn't know where she was.

For some reason, this news cracked me up. All I could think of was *Weekend at Bernie's*. Alex and I could picture her, our Queenie, propped up in some corner of the hospital with a gin and tonic, watching as nurses and doctors scurried around trying to find her, the center of attention just like she liked.

That was the first laugh of many that week as we remembered all of the wonderful stories of my mom. We laughed as much as we cried, maybe even more, thus proving the whole concept of this devotional: Goodness and God are always present in life's ups and downs, we just have to pay attention.

What follows is the closing of my tribute to my mama at her funeral. I pray her lesson impacts your life and your heart as much as she impacted mine.

***

My mom's last lesson is truly the most important: She taught me that God is always with us.

Now, my mom didn't teach me this in an in your face kind of way. While she went to church almost every Sunday for most of her life, she wasn't one to go around quoting scripture or singing praise songs. She taught me this lesson through matter-of-fact conversations woven into life experiences.

The first time I remember having a serious conversation on this topic was in 1991 when I was playing Garth Brooks' *Unanswered Prayers* on repeat. After about the fourth time the song came on, she looked over and said, "I really don't like this song."

Shocked that anyone would have the audacity to speak ill of Garth, I promptly asked, "Well, why in the world not?"

I will never forget her answer.

She said, "Katherine, our prayers never go unanswered. God may answer *No* or *Not yet*, but you should know He will always answer them in His time."

While I didn't really appreciate her explanation then, the more I live and the more I pray, the more I know her words to be true.

Another memory that is cemented in my mind occurred when I was in college. I was the New Member Educator for my sorority, and one of my jobs was to create the get to know you books the new members would receive. Each older member had a page in the book where she introduced herself through pictures, quotes, and fun facts about herself. Over Christmas, Mom helped me make copies of all the pages and put the books together.

As we worked, I noticed her getting more and more disturbed. Finally, she looked up and said, "Shugah, why do all of these girls say they love Diet Coke and Jesus? You do not love those two things the same way. They are *not* equal."

Now, y'all, this was shocking coming from a woman who drank a Caffeine Free Diet Coke almost every day of her adult life.

But she was adamant I understand that the love we have for Jesus, and more importantly, the love He has for us, is much bigger and deeper and stronger than any feelings we have for a 12 ounce can of soda.

Finally, the memory that stands out the most is a conversation we had while driving to Kentucky when I was in college. I have no idea why we were even going there, but I vividly remember being on a highway in the Tennessee mountains and talking about how I could totally understand why ancient people worshipped the sun because it impacted everything they did, and we shouldn't judge them for not believing in our God. Was this crazy philosophy driven by my recent religions of the world class? Was I just young and naïve? I don't know.

Mom just kinda looked at me like bless your heart and said, "I guess I can see why you might say that. You've never been in a position where you felt so alone and knew God was the only one holding your hand."

You see, in 1978, my mom had to make some tough choices. Choices that I'm sure brought fear and doubt and uncertainty. She ultimately made the decision to become a single mom in a time and a place that wasn't always supportive of unwed mothers. This decision included a move from South Carolina to Colorado, which left her completely separated from the family and friends she loved so much.

I had always thought that my mom's time in Denver, followed by her new start in Rock Hill and her determination to be the best mom possible, were powered mainly by her own courage and resolve, as well as a little bit of that Smith stubbornness we're both known for. But after that conversation, I realized she didn't see it like that. She had no idea how things were going to work out, but she knew exactly who was with her and who would carry her through.

As I was writing this tribute Wednesday night, when I got to this point, I knew I wanted to include a piece of scripture, but I couldn't quite figure out which one. Thursday morning I awoke to a text from a dear friend who shared Psalm 139, and as soon as I read it, I knew it was the perfect verse.

Psalm 139:7-10 reads: *Where can I go from your Spirit? Where can I flee from your presence? If I go up to the heavens, you are there; if I make my bed in the depths, you are there. If I rise on the wings of the dawn, if I settle on the far side of the sea, even there your hand will guide me, your right hand will hold me fast.*

The reminder of this verse just when I needed it most is simply one more example of God's continual presence in our lives. In the parties and celebrations, in the challenges and the choices, God is always with us. It doesn't matter where we go, across the country or right around the block, from the cradle to the grave, God's love will sustain us every step of the way.

I know this to be true because my mama said it, but even more so because she lived it. May we all strive to do the same.

Acknowledgements

To Sherry (aka Shirley) for asking, "Well, why don't you?" when I casually mentioned I wanted to start a blog. Without those four little words six years ago, I probably wouldn't be writing these acknowledgements today, so thank you for being a good Mama J and pushing me out of the nest.

To Emily, Caroline, Anna, and Margaret for believing in me from day one, for calling me on the phone, for hugging me tight, for showing up, and for never taking no for an answer.

To Elizabeth, Lilla, Leslie, Courtney, Christine, and Graham for the laughter, for being the sisters I never had, and for being the hands and feet of Jesus to me and so many others.

To my Furman Girls for always being willing to hang out with Pappy, for celebrating each other's milestones, for carrying each other through tough times, and for giving me grace when I get behind on Marco Polo.

To my Rock Thrill Girls for seeing me through questionable fashion decisions, for walking up and down Broadway to find me a mechanical bull, and for loving me so well for so many years.

To Cathy, the best of both worlds, for never getting angry when I stole your antenna, for being as directionally challenged as I am, and for making the flight. I can never thank you enough for that, but I will continually strive to pay your love and friendship forward.

To Dottie for giving me space for all of my verbal processing and questioning, for pushing me to use my voice and stand up for others, and for understanding the algorithm.

To Carter for encouraging me, for making me laugh with your cheesy dad jokes, and for being a daily witness to the power of God's redeeming love.

To Kayla for always spilling the tea and for cultivating in me the belief that my stories and experiences can help others. I love ya, friend, but I will never love John Mayer.

To my Foundation Family for strengthening my walk by sharing yours week after week. Each one of you has inspired me in some kind of way, and I'm so thankful to be a part of our class.

To Ruthie for being relentless in your pursuit of volunteers, for setting the manicure bar high, and for giving me multiple opportunities to use my gifts, serve others, and grow in my faith.

To Irene for challenging me to write my morning pages, for believing in my dream, for opening your home and your heart to all of us, and for using your own gifts to motivate and love the women around you. I can't wait to read your book!

To Myra Davis Branic for loving my boys at After Care even when they're feisty and for sharing your publishing wisdom right there in the parking lot. You are proof that God places people in our lives for a reason.

To Grims for being the best Prom ticket taker in the tri-state area, for giving me weekly Instagram encouragement, and for being a joyful light to so many.

To Mittie Beth for giving the best hugs, for cheering me on week after week, and for understanding the special grandmom-mom-only daughter bond the way few others can. Watch out for those treadmills!

To my loyal blog followers for being here since the beginning of this adventure, for the likes, for the shares, but mainly for the love. Y'all are the best, and I appreciate your support more than you know!

To you, my readers, for making it to the end. Thank you for trusting me enough to give this book a chance. I hope you've gained at least a little grain of truth from reading it, and I hope you continue to laugh and love, even during the hard times.

To Jackson, Reeves, and Brooks for giving the best snuggles, for making me laugh even when I don't want to, for helping me be a better person, for always saving me the last bite, and for teaching me more about God than anyone else ever has.

And to Alex for believing in me even when I didn't believe in myself, for being my rock and my teddy bear, for taking my advice and growing your hair out, for reading every post and giving me feedback (even though you're not my target audience), and for always wanting to hold my hand.

About the Author

Katherine Bryant is a wife, mom, teacher, daughter, and friend just trying to figure out who she is, what she wants to be when she grows up, and where God is leading her. A graduate of Furman University and the University of South Carolina, she loves a cozy hooded sweatshirt, Papermate Flair pens, and a little coffee in her creamer.

Known for laughing at inappropriate times, Katherine loves to entertain her family and friends with a good story. Her ultimate goal is to remind us that God is always with us, all we have to do is pay attention. She lives with her husband and sons in Columbia, SC.

Be sure to follow her on Instagram @Laughsatfunerals and on her blog, Katherine-Bryant.com.